POLAN GUIDE 2024

CORY R. HOBBS

POLAND MAP

Copyright © 2023 [Cory R. Hobbs]

All rights reserved. Except for brief quotations included in critical reviews and certain other noncommercial uses allowed by copyright law, no part of this publication may be reproduced, distributed, or transmitted in any form or by any means, including photocopying, recording, or other electronic or mechanical methods, without the prior written permission of the copyright holder.

CONTENTS

POLAND MAP..2
INTRODUCTION... 5
Chapter One: Welcome to Poland...............8
Chapter Two: How to get there................12
    Essentials Travel informations............... 12
    Visa Requirements................................... 12
Chapter Three: Navigating Poland............21
    Transportation Guide................................ 21
    When to Go...32
Chapter Four: Poland top Destinations...................36
    Accommodations...................................... 36
    Warsaw capital and Extravaganza.........39
    Krakow: A Historical Tour:........................41
Chapter Five: Cultural Immersion..........................44
    Polish Tradition and Customs:................ 44
    Events and festivals in 2024................... 46
    Polish Delights: Must-Try Recipes.......... 51
Chapter Six: Historical Landmark............................54
    Royal Castles and Palaces...................... 54
Chapter Seven: Outdoor Adventures...................... 61
    Exploring Poland's National Parks..........61
    Nature Trails and Hiking.......................... 65
    Activities with Water................................68
Chapter Eighth: Local Experience........................... 73

Shopping for Souvenirs.. 73
Getting Along with Locals.. 79
Chapter Nine: Practical Tips..82
Safety Guidelines..82
Information about Health and Emergencies........... 85
Essentials for Packing... 89
CONCLUSION...93

INTRODUCTION

Welcome to the fascinating country of Poland, where modernism blends with history and breathtaking scenery appears around every corner. This travel book is your reliable travel companion as you set off on your adventure through this fascinating nation in 2024, offering advice, suggestions, and vital details to make your stay nothing short of spectacular.

We will discover the cultural diversity of Krakow, stroll through the energetic streets of Warsaw, and take in the seaside appeal of Gdansk in the pages that follow. This book has something to offer every type of tourist, be they a history buff keen to learn about Poland's colorful past, a nature lover looking for peace and quiet in the Tatra Mountains, or a foodie ready to indulge in the delectable Polish cuisine.

As we open the chapters, you'll find useful advice on getting around, an understanding of regional traditions and customs, and a well selected list of places you simply must see. Poland in 2024 is an entire experience that is simply waiting to be discovered, not merely a place to travel to.

So buckle in, and allow us to transport you virtually through the heart of Europe. Poland welcomes you with open arms, promising a tapestry of history, culture, and natural beauty that will leave an enduring impression on your travel memories, whether you're a seasoned tourist returning to explore more.

Chapter One: Welcome to Poland

Poland invites you to discover its varied landscapes, from the busy cityscapes of Warsaw to the timeless elegance of Krakow's Old Town, in this warm and inviting embrace of history. Poland is a place that appeals to all types of travelers, be they fascinated by the minute details of historic sites or the tranquil beauty of natural wonders.

The secret to discovering Poland's wonders in 2024 is this trip guide. Flip through the pages to find the hidden treasures, taste the flavors of authentic Polish food, and become engrossed in the colorful culture that characterizes this fascinating country.

So let hospitality be your guide as you set out on your journey. Welcome to Poland, a nation that beckons you to immerse yourself in its history, feel its warmth, and make lifelong memories.

What's New for Cutting-Edge Cultural Events in 2024?

Take in cutting-edge shows, installations, and cultural events that highlight Poland's contemporary artistic energy. A boundary-pushing cultural landscape is anticipated in 2024, along with interactive displays and modern galleries.

New Technologies in Travel:
Utilize the newest travel technology to navigate with ease. Useful applications that provide up-to-date information on events, transit, and must-see sights will help you stay in touch. With the help of interactive maps and augmented reality instructions, see Poland like never before.

Environmentally Friendly Projects: Poland is dedicated to sustainability. Learn about green travel choices, environmentally friendly lodging, and programs to protect the nation's natural beauty. Come along with the push toward eco-friendly travel and adventure.

Adventures in gastronomic Arts: Savor Poland's current gastronomic revolution. Anticipate delectable new dishes that combine classic flavors with creative twists. Savor the changing flavors of Polish cuisine at anything from street food markets to cutting-edge dining establishments.

Undiscovered Treasures Away from the beaten Path: Explore areas not as well-traveled and unearth lesser-known treasures. Undiscovered gems, charming towns, and unspoiled scenery await the adventurous voyager to discover in 2024.

Travel Adventures with a Theme:
Customize your trip by booking themed lodgings. Whether you love the outdoors, history, or urban exploration, there are tours and activities tailored to your interests that offer a more in-depth look at Poland's core.

Retreats for Well-Being and Leisure:
Relax in Poland's spa destinations. Prioritize self-care amidst the diverse tapestry of your travel experiences, from yoga and meditation sessions to spa vacations in picturesque rural settings.

We'll walk you through the most recent and interesting changes in this area, so that your discovery of Poland in 2024 is more than just a visit—it's a vibrant, modern experience that embodies the times.

Chapter Two: How to get there

Essentials Travel informations

Visa Requirements

It is imperative that you are aware of the exact visa requirements before departing on your trip to Poland in 2024.

Visa Exemptions: For brief visits, citizens of some nations may not need to apply for a visa. Verify the duration of stay and whether your nationality qualifies for a visa exemption.

Membership in the Schengen Area: Poland is a part of the Schengen Area. Possessing a Schengen visa usually entitles you to unrestricted travel throughout Poland and other Schengen nations. Make sure your visa is valid forthe reason and length of your stay.

Visa Types:
Find out what kind of travel visa you will require. Business, student, and tourist visas are examples of common classifications. Select the one that best fits the reason for your trip.

Application Process: Start applying for a visa far in advance of the dates you want to travel. To get the required application forms and information, get in touch with the Polish consulate or embassy in your nation.

Essential Records:
A valid passport, filled-out application papers, passport-sized pictures, a travel itinerary, confirmation of your lodging, and evidence of your ability to pay for your stay should all be included in your packet of documents.

Evidence of Travel Insurance: Proof of travel insurance that pays for emergencies and medical costs is often required for visa applications. Make sure your insurance policy satisfies the requirements.

Visa Fees: Understand the payment options and associated fees when applying for a visa. When submitting your application, make sure you pay the necessary fees, and save the receipt for your records.

Processing Time: Recognize how long visa applications normally take to process. Send in your paperwork well in advance to allow for unforeseen hold-ups.

Interviews and Biometrics: Certain visa categories might call for the gathering of biometric information or an interview. Arrive on time for any appointments that the embassy or consulate may have set.

Look for any updates:

Always stay informed about any changes to the conditions for obtaining a visa. For up-to-date information, you can trust the official website of the Polish consulate or embassy in your nation.

To guarantee that your visa application is approved, check with the proper authorities and offer accurate and comprehensive documents. Keep in mind that the requirements for obtaining a visa can change depending on your country of citizenship and the reason for your travel. Happy travels!

Money and Financial Concerns

The official currency of Poland is the Polish Złoty (PLN). Learn about the current exchange rate so that you may make wise financial decisions.

Exchange of Currency:

For the best rates, exchange money at banks or authorized currency exchange offices (kantor). Steer clear of unlicensed street exchange services to guarantee honest dealings.

ATMs: Accepting major credit and debit cards, ATMs are widely distributed in urban areas. To prevent any problems with card usage overseas, inquire with your bank about foreign transaction costs and let them know when you will be traveling.

Visa and MasterCard credit cards are commonly accepted in hotels, restaurants, and other larger facilities. Tell your bank about your trip schedule to avoid any issues with using your card.

Use of Cash: Although credit and debit cards are widely accepted, it's a good idea to have some cash on hand for little purchases, local markets, or establishments that might not take them.

Tipping Etiquette: In Poland, it is traditional to leave a tip. If there is no service charge, it is customary to tip between 10% and 15% at restaurants. It's also traditional to tip tour guides and taxi drivers.

Creating a budget: Take Poland's cost of living into consideration. Do some research on average costs for lodging, meals, travel, and activities to make sure you have enough money for the trip.

Emergency Cash: Maintain a modest emergency cash reserve as well as a credit card. This can come in handy in the event of unforeseen circumstances or if you find yourself in a place where there are few ways to make payments.

Banking Hours: Know the hours that banks are open, particularly if you must physically visit one. Most banks are open Monday through Friday, with some having restricted hours on Saturdays.

Security Procedures:

Keep your PIN and cards secure. For protection against loss or theft, think about carrying a money belt or a safe travel wallet.

By keeping yourself informed and making advance plans, you'll be ready to enjoy your time in Poland and handle your money wisely. A thorough understanding of currencies and money matters improves the entire travel experience, whether you're visiting historical sites, sampling local food, or shopping for trinkets.

Spoken Word

Although many people in tourist areas and larger cities speak English, particularly the younger generation, it is nevertheless good to learn a few basic Polish phrases. The official language of Poland is Polish.Simple Polish Expressions:

Get familiar with basic salutations such as "Dzień dobry" (good morning), "Dziękuję" (thank you), and "Proszę" (please). Gaining an understanding of these fundamentals will greatly improve your communication.

Proficiency in English:
English is widely spoken by hotel employees, restaurant servers, and other hospitality industry professionals in popular tourist locations. Smaller towns and off-the-beaten-path areas may have less proficient English speakers, though.

Translation applications: For precise and timely communication, make use of translation applications. You can translate spoken and written words with apps like Google Translate, which makes navigating menus and signs simpler.

Visit Tourist Information Centers: Ask for help from the multilingual staff who can direct you, provide you maps, and address any questions you may have.

Discover Important Place Names:
Learn the names of the locations you intend to visit. When requesting directions or transportation, it can be useful.

Public Transportation Signs: To use public transportation systems, you must be aware of the fundamental symbols and signs used. In larger cities, English is also used for most signage.

Cultural Sensitivity: When communicating, be mindful of cultural quirks. Polite and courteous relationships are valued by Poles. It is traditional to address persons with their rightful titles (Pan/Pani).

Local Dialects: You may come across regional dialects or variations of the Polish language in various parts of Poland. Accept the differences and try to pick up a few native words.

Emergency Expressions: Be familiar with crucial emergency expressions, such as how to request aid or locate medical support. In an emergency, knowing basic medical terminology and figures can be quite helpful.

Language Exchange: Take into account taking part in language exchange initiatives or making connections with locals who have a desire to share languages. It's a fantastic opportunity to meet new people and advance your Polish.

Even if there can be some minor language barriers, communicating with Poles will surely be enjoyable due to their warmth and kindness. Your time in Poland will be enhanced if you take advantage of the chance to become familiar with the language and customs of the region.

Chapter Three: Navigating Poland

Transportation Guide

Air Travel:

Major Airports: Warsaw Chopin Airport (WAW) is the largest of Poland's multiple international airports. Gdańsk Lech Wałęsa Airport (GDN) and Kraków John Paul II International Airport (KRK) are two more important airports.

Trains: InterCity Services: Poland's InterCity trains provide rapid and comfortable travel between major cities. It is advised to purchase tickets in advance, particularly during periods of high travel demand.

Regional Trains: Traveling across neighboring towns and cities on a regional train is a great idea. They frequently provide better prices and gorgeous views of the surrounding area.

Buses: Popular long-distance bus services that connect major cities and even neighboring countries are FlixBus and PolskiBus. Online reservations are available for tickets.

Local Buses: Taking public transportation within cities and villages might be an affordable option. Routes and timetables are typically available online or at bus stations.

City trams are available in several Polish cities, such as Warsaw and Krakow. These networks are quite effective. Trams are an easy way to get to different districts and visit city centers.

Metro in Warsaw Metro: The only metro system in Poland is in Warsaw. One efficient and dependable method of getting around the city is via the metro.

Car Rentals: Hiring a car gives you more freedom if you want to travel via smaller towns or rural areas. Poland is home to several large international vehicle rental firms.

Taxis: Taxi Services: In cities, taxis are widely accessible. For a dependable and reasonably priced service, use ridesharing applications or trustworthy taxi firms.

Cycling: Renting a bike is possible in a lot of cities, particularly popular tourist spots. Riding a bike across Poland is a fantastic way to take in the landscape.

Walking: Pedestrian-Friendly Cities: With well-kept sidewalks and pedestrian zones, Polish cities are frequently pedestrian-friendly. Strolling around town is a great way to find hidden treasures and take in the local vibe.

Travel Apps: Transportation Apps: For up-to-date information on routes, schedules, and delays, use transportation apps. Apps like Google Maps and Jakdojade (for public transit) are useful resources.

Check for any travel updates before you go, especially on holidays or during busy times of the year. Poland's well-functioning transportation system makes it easy to discover the varied landscapes and cultural treasures of this stunning nation. Happy travels!

Major Airports:
Warsaw Chopin Airport (WAW): The busiest and largest airport, offering a huge selection of international flights, is located in the capital city.
Kraków Southern Poland is served by John Paul II International Airport (KRK), a major hub for both local and international travel.

Gdańsk Lech Wałęsa Airport (GDN): Situated in the north, it offers easy access to the region surrounding the Baltic Sea.
Regional Airports: To facilitate travel to particular locations, Poland maintains a number of regional airports in addition to its major airports, including Wrocław Nicolaus Copernicus Airport (WRO) and Katowice International Airport (KTW).
Airlines: LOT Polish Airlines, Ryanair, Wizz Air, and other domestic and foreign airlines are among those that fly in Poland. Select airlines according to your spending limit and favored routes.
Scheduling: Make sure you plan and reserve your flights well in advance, particularly during the busiest travel times. To evaluate costs and locate the best offers, use internet resources and travel companies.

Domestic flights are accessible for those looking for a quicker option, even though Poland is well-connected by road and rail. Based on your plan, look for direct flights or efficient connections.

Airport Amenities: Duty-free stores, dining options, lounges, and currency exchange services are among the contemporary amenities available at Polish airports. To take use of these services and guarantee a stress-free travel experience, arrive early.

Travel to and from airports: Taxis, shuttle services, and public transit are among the easy ways to get to and from major airports. Airports can be reached directly by train from many cities.

Immigration and Customs:

When you arrive, be informed of the immigration and customs processes. Make sure you have all the paperwork you need for your trip, such as a current passport and any necessary visas.

Security Procedures: Observe airport security guidelines. Be mindful of the rules governing liquids, electronics, and other things in your carry-on bags, and give yourself enough of time for security procedures.

Updates on flights:

Keep track on the status of your flight. When making a reservation, make sure you have the correct contact information on file and keep an eye out for any changes on cancellations or delays.

COVID-19 Points to Remember:

Stay informed about any health precautions or travel restrictions pertaining to the current world situation. For the most recent information, check with airlines and official government sources.

Traveling by flight is a practical and effective method to see the various landscapes and cultural treasures that Poland has to offer, whether you're traveling inside the nation or just arriving. Happy travels!

Buses and Trains

Trains: InterCity Services: Poland's InterCity (IC) trains provide a convenient and quick means of transportation between major cities. Get your tickets in advance, especially when travel demand is high.

Regional Trains: Regional trains offer links to cities and smaller communities. These trains are reasonably priced and provide beautiful views of the Polish countryside.

Purchasing train tickets can be done via mobile apps, online, or at train stations. For the most recent timetables and reservations, check for the Polish State Railways' (PKP Intercity) official website or mobile apps.

Poland's high-speed rail network is currently undergoing expansion. To travel more quickly, look for high-speed connections between large cities.

Rail Passes: A rail pass can save you money if you want to take frequent train travels. Different pass choices are offered to accommodate different travel schedules.

Comfort Classes: There are various classes available on trains, such as first class and standard. First-class tickets come with additional room for amenities and seating.

Train Stations: Central train stations in major cities feature amenities like baggage services, waiting areas, and ticket counters. For a seamless experience, heed the announcements and signs at the station.

Popular long-distance bus services that connect major cities and even neighboring countries are PolskiBus and FlixBus. Purchase your tickets online and keep an eye out for adaptable travel options.

Local Buses: Public buses offer an inexpensive form of transportation within cities and villages. Local timetables and routes can be found online or at bus stations.

Bus Terminals: Long-distance and international buses arrive and depart from central bus terminals located in cities. These terminals have stores, ticket counters, and waiting lounges, among other services.

Bus tickets can be purchased online or at bus terminals in advance. While some buses do accept payments on board, it is best to have a ticket in advance, particularly during peak travel times.

Express Services:

"Ekspres" or "Express" buses, sometimes referred to as express buses, offer quicker connections between major cities. Travel times are shortened by the frequent less stops on these services.

Comfort Features: Wi-Fi, power outlets, and roomier seats are just a few of the amenities that certain bus operators provide. Verify the available amenities when purchasing your ticket.

Buses are essential for establishing connections between rural communities. Buses connect you to scenic rural areas if you want to venture to less-traveled spots.

Poland's well-developed transportation networks guarantee that you can easily and conveniently take in the splendor of the nation, whether you prefer to travel by bus or train. When traveling through Poland, make sure to check schedules, plan your itineraries ahead of time, and enjoy the variety of sceneries. Happy travels!

Tips for Local Transportation

Public Transportation: Buses and Trams: A lot of cities have large bus and tram networks, notably Warsaw and Krakow. Using public transit is an affordable method to go around the city. Get tickets via mobile apps, internet, or kiosks.

Travel Cards: Take into consideration buying travel cards, or city cards, which provide limitless access to public transit for a predetermined amount of time. These cards frequently come with other perks, such museum admission discounts.

There is only one metro system in Poland, and that is the Warsaw metro. When commuting within the city, the metro is quite effective, especially during rush hour.

Taxi Services: Reliable Businesses To guarantee reasonable rates and a secure travel, use trustworthy taxi services or ride-sharing applications. Seek out authorized taxi stalls or make reservations using reputable applications.

Bicycles: Renting a bike is a common practice in many places, encouraging environmentally friendly transportation. Take your time exploring the city and take use of the designated bike lanes in some cities.

Walking: Pedestrian Zones: Poland's cities have a lot of pedestrian zones, which makes strolling in the downtown areas enjoyable. It's advisable to wear comfortable shoes, especially when visiting ancient areas.

Tickets and Card Organizations:

Validation: To prevent fines, make sure your ticket or card is valid before boarding a public transportation vehicle. It could be necessary for you to show proof of purchase at the metro station entrance in certain cities, such as Warsaw.

Cultural Courtesies:

Queuing: When boarding a tram or bus, line up at the appropriate stops. In public transit, orderly and courteous behavior is valued by Polish people.

Timetables and Schedules:

Make a Plan: Prior to traveling, review the timetables and schedules, particularly for buses and trams. To prevent getting lost, be informed of the final departure timings.

Help with Language: Consult the Locals Never be afraid to ask for assistance from locals if you have any questions about routes or transit specifics. In general, Poles are amiable and eager to help.

Safety Measures:

Remain Alert: Pay attention to your surroundings, particularly in crowded areas. When traveling at night, be sure to choose well-lit stops and keep a watch on your valuables.

Easily Achievable Options:

Availability: whether you have trouble moving around, find out whether there are any accessible transportation choices available. Certain cities have trams and buses with low floors.

Making the most of your trips within Polish cities and villages is easy when you know how to use the country's local transportation system. The local transit alternatives provide an easy way to take in Poland's splendor, whether you're visiting ancient sites, bustling markets, or quaint suburbs.

When to Go

(April to June): Blooming Landscapes: Spring is a great time to go for those who enjoy the outdoors because it delivers bright greenery and blooming flowers. Gardens and parks spring to life, and the weather is comfortable and mild.

Festivals and Events: The spring season offers a plethora of opportunities to immerse oneself in Poland's rich cultural heritage.

Summer (June to August): Mild Weather: With its pleasant temperatures, particularly in July and August, summer is the busiest travel season. It's a great season for festivals, city exploration, and outdoor activities.

Festivals & Events: The summer months bring with them a plethora of outdoor activities, music festivals, and cultural celebrations.

Autumn (September to November): Mild Weather: There are less people and nice weather in September and early October. See how the leaves in parks and woodlands change color in the fall.

Wine Harvest: In places like Lower Silesia, the fall harvest is when wine is harvested. Think about going to vineyards to sample wine and take in the beautiful scenery.

Winter (December to February): Winter Wonderland: Visit Poland in the wintertime if you like winter activities and lively environments. There is good skiing in the Tatra Mountains.

Christmas Markets: Take in the charming Christmas markets with their traditional delicacies, festive décor, and handcrafted products in places like Krakow and Warsaw.

Early autumn and late spring are the shoulder seasons.

Reduced Crowds and Milder Weather: It is best to visit in late spring (May) or early fall (September) to avoid the crowds and enjoy nice weather. It's a great time of year for outdoor activities and tourism.

Taking into account

Peak Travel Season: The busiest months, particularly in well-known tourist locations, are July and August. During this time, schedule your activities and lodging in advance.

Benefits of Traveling Off-Peak: Winter and shoulder seasons might provide more relaxed travel conditions and cheaper hotel costs.

Events Calendar: Cultural Events: Look through the calendar to find festivals, celebrations, and cultural events that interest you. Poland holds a number of events all year long.

Holidays in the area:

Public Holidays: When making travel plans, take into account regional holidays. On some public holidays, some services and attractions can be closed or have increased traffic.

The ideal time to travel to Poland ultimately depends on your interests and the experiences you hope to have. Poland has a wide variety of possibilities all year long, whether you're interested in winter sports, cultural events, or outdoor activities.

Chapter Four: Poland top Destinations

Accommodations

Poland provides a large selection of lodging options to accommodate different tastes and price ranges. In Poland,

Hotels:

There is a wide variety of hotels in Poland, ranging from opulent properties in large cities to more affordable options and tiny boutique hotels. All around the nation, there are both locally owned and international hotel chains to choose from.

Bed & Breakfasts and guesthouses are smaller, frequently family-run accommodations that offer a more individualized experience. They provide a warm and welcoming ambiance and can be found in both urban and rural settings.

Hostels: Especially well-liked by younger and more frugal tourists, hostels offer shared lodging in the form of dormitories with shared amenities. Also, a lot of hostels have private rooms.

Holiday Apartments: Renting apartments or vacation houses is a common option, especially for people who are going to be traveling in a group or for extended periods. Numerous possibilities are available through local agencies and websites like Airbnb.

Agritourism: Guests staying on farms or in rural residences might locate agritourism accommodations in rural locations. This offers an opportunity to savor locally grown, fresh vegetables and experience traditional country living.

Poland boasts a multitude of historically significant castles and palaces that have been transformed into hotels. Remaining in one of these accommodations provides a distinctive and frequently opulent experience.

Spa and Wellness Resorts: Poland is well-known for its spa towns, and the country has a large number of wellness-oriented resorts. These frequently consist of natural resource-based therapies, wellness centers, and thermal baths.
Mountain Huts: Mountain huts, also known as schroniska, are located in mountainous areas, particularly in the Tatra Mountains. These are simple lodging options that provide a spot to dine and rest during mountain hikes for hikers and outdoor enthusiasts.
Campsites: Throughout Poland, there are caravan parks and campgrounds for outdoor enthusiasts. They are frequently located in picturesque settings, offering a more intimate encounter with the natural world.

Think about things like location, price range, and the kind of experience you want when selecting a place to stay. While there are many alternatives available in large cities like Warsaw, Krakow, and Gdansk, smaller towns and rural places offer special chances to get in touch with the local way of life and natural surroundings.

Warsaw capital and Extravaganza

Poland's largest and capital city, Warsaw, is well-known for its lively culture, fascinating history, and exciting events.

History:

The Warsaw Uprising during World War II and the post-war reconstruction are just two of the important moments in the city's lengthy and complicated history.

Culture: With a large number of museums, theaters, and galleries, the city is a center for the arts. Notable cultural attractions are the POLIN Museum of the History of Polish Jews, Wilanów Palace, and the Royal Castle.

Architecture: Warsaw features a diverse range of architectural styles, including modern, contemporary, and Gothic and Renaissance. One of the best examples of medieval architecture is the Old Town, which is recognized as a UNESCO World Heritage Site.

Parks & Green Spaces: Residents and visitors can enjoy recreational spaces in a number of parks in Warsaw, such as Łazienki Park and Wilanów Palace Park.

Events:

The Warsaw International Film Festival is a yearly film festival that presents an eclectic array of global films.

Chopin Concerts: Frédéric Chopin, the well-known composer, was born in Warsaw, and his music is performed in concerts all year long.

Events Celebrating Multiculturalism: Warsaw holds a number of events that highlight its multiculturalism and represent the diversity of its people.

Warsaw organizes cultural festivals all year round, which include literature events, art exhibitions, and music festivals.

Nightlife: There are lots of pubs, clubs, and entertainment venues in the city, which boasts a thriving nightlife culture.

Krakow: A Historical Tour:

Historical Significance: Known for its medieval architecture and historical sites, Krakow is one of Poland's oldest and most important cities.

Royal Capital: From 1038 to 1569, it was Poland's capital and the home of the country's monarchs. Standing on a hill, the Wawel Castle represents Krakow's regal past.

Old Town (Stare Miasto): With its quaint cobblestone alleys, market squares, and historic buildings, Krakow's Old Town is a UNESCO World Heritage Site.

Several Polish rulers and national heroes are buried at Wawel Cathedral, a notable monument inside Wawel Castle.

Jewish Quarter (Kazimierz): A neighborhood full of synagogues, museums, and a bustling street life, Kazimierz is renowned for its rich Jewish history and culture.

Rynek Główny, also known as Main Market Square, is the center of Krakow and is encircled by shops, cafes, and historic buildings. It's among Europe's biggest medieval squares.

Culture and Events:

The annual international film festival Krakow Film Festival presents independent and avant-garde films.

Krakow Christmas Market: Located in the Main Market Square, this lively market offers traditional crafts, delectable cuisine, and a happy vibe.

The Krakow Literary Festival draws authors and readers from all over the world as it honors literature and writers.

Krakow is home to a number of music festivals, showcasing jazz, contemporary, and classical genres.

Cultural Museums: The National Museum, which has a sizable collection of Polish art, is one of Krakow's many museums.

Krakow is a fascinating destination because of its unique combination of history, culture, and exciting events. Please let me know if you have any special queries or if there's anything in particular about Krakow that interests you.

Chapter Five: Cultural Immersion

Polish Tradition and Customs:

Poland's rich cultural past and history are essential to the country's traditions and customs. An overview of several.
The following lists some well-known Polish customs:
Monday of Easter - Śmigus-Dyngus: On this day, it is traditional for people to playfully splash water on one another as a symbol of purification and hygiene. It's a joyful and vibrant celebration.
Christmas Eve - Wigilia: The most important day of the holiday season in Poland is Christmas Eve. To celebrate, families gather for a meal known as "Wigilia," which consists of twelve traditional dishes, each of which represents one of the twelve apostles.
A fun tradition known as Pączki Day is celebrated on Fat Thursday (Tłusty Czwartek), the day before Lent begins in earnest. Pączki, which are deep-fried dough pastries filled with jam or other delectable fillings, are enjoyed on this day.
Every Saint's Day - All Saints: Poles visit cemeteries, light candles, and pay respects to their deceased loved ones on this November 1st event. It's a day to honor and commemorate the lives of those who have passed away.

People celebrate St. Andrew's Day, or Andrzejki, on November 29th evening by doing various divination and fortune-telling rituals. It's a fun superstitious tradition.
The distinctive embroidery from the Kaszuby area is widely recognized and is often found on traditional clothing. This regional custom is typified by the intricate decorations and vibrant colors.

Traditional folk music and dance traditions are abundant in Poland. Dance methods vary according on the region, and instruments such as the violin, clarinet, and accordion are often featured in the music.

Polish Weddings:

Weddings in Poland are usually multi-day, extravagant affairs. Traditional practices include things like the breaking of bread, blessings for the marriage, and other symbolic ceremonies.

An annual celebration of prosperity and good fortune, the Lajkonik Festival in Krakow is typified by a parade led by an individual dressed as the Lajkonik, a bearded man astride a wooden horse.

Smigus-Dyngus Parade: There are parades and festivities around Śmigus-Dyngus, particularly in Krakow. Participants participate in water fights and parades while wearing traditional costumes.

These are only a few examples of the wide variety of traditions and rituals that exist in Poland. The unique customs that may exist in each place contribute to the nation's richness and diversity of culture.

Events and festivals in 2024

Warmth and Hospitality: Visitors Are Respected: Polish culture is firmly rooted in hospitality. Visitors are accorded the highest level of respect, and hosts frequently go above and beyond to ensure their comfort.

Salutations:
Cordial Salutations: Making direct eye contact and giving a solid handshake are standard greetings. When addressing persons in formal settings, titles like "Pan" (Mr.) or "Pani" (Mrs.) are frequently used.
Honoring Name Days:
Celebrate Name Day: Many Poles commemorate their name day, which is the feast day of the saint after whom they were named, in addition to their birthdays. It's a momentous event, and greetings are given.

Gift-Giving Etiquette: Thoughtful Presents: It is customary to open gifts in front of the giver as a sign of appreciation. Gifts like wine, chocolates, and flowers are typical. A funeral is often connected with an even amount of flowers, so steer clear of that.

Family Principles:
Embroidered Families: Polish culture places a strong emphasis on the family. Sundays are typically used for traditional meals and family get-togethers. Strong family bonds and respect for elders are highly prized.
Easter customs:
Rmigus-Dyngus: A fun custom known as Śmigus-Dyngus is people jokingly splattering water on one another on Easter Monday. It represents purification and prosperity.

Christmas customs:
Wigilia: Wigilia, or Christmas Eve, is a unique day. Families get together to celebrate with a twelve-course dinner that represents the Twelve Apostles. The Christmas wafer (opłatek) is broken to start the meal.
Polish folklore: Poland possesses an abundant legacy of folk music, dance, and traditional costumes. These customs' regional variants highlight the richness of the nation's cultural legacy.
Religious Observances: Religious festivities: Religious festivities are connected to a number of Polish customs. Rituals, processions, and pilgrimages are all essential components of the cultural calendar.

Nature and Folk Beliefs:

Poles frequently uphold customs connected to natural cycles and have a great regard for the natural world. In many areas, traditional beliefs and customs pertaining to the natural world are still common.

Dining Protocol:
Table etiquette: It is customary to wait for the host to begin serving when you are dining. It's also tradition to consume all that is on your platter. During meals, toasts are customary, and it is courteous to respond.
Pączki Day:
Thursday Fat: Pączki Day, which is observed on the final Thursday before Lent, is all about indulging on pączki, a kind of Polish doughnut.
You can establish a connection with the core of Polish culture by adopting these customs. Participating in joyous festivities, dining with locals, or feeling the warmth of Polish hospitality are just a few examples of how these traditions add to a fully complete travel experience.

Events &Festivals
Wianki is a traditional midsummer event celebrated in June that includes dancing, music, and the floating of flower wreaths on waterways. Krakow and Warsaw are frequently the sites of important events.
Jazz at the July Odra Festival:

This jazz festival, held in Wrocław, draws both local and international jazz musicians. For fans of jazz, it's a major cultural occasion.

July's Open'er Festival:
Open'er Festival, one of the biggest music gatherings in Poland, is held in Gdynia and offers a wide range of Polish and foreign performers performing in different genres.

Malta Festiwal (June - August):
Festiwal Malta is a multidisciplinary arts festival that takes place in Poznań and includes creative events, concerts, and theater performances.

May/June: Krakow Film Festival: Among the oldest film festivals in Europe, this event features a broad selection of documentaries, short films, and animated pictures.

Warsaw Autumn (September): World-class Polish and international composers and performers play at this contemporary classical music festival in Warsaw.

Pierogi Festival (August): In honor of Poland's national dish, pierogis, this festival in Krakow provides a range of fillings and styles for attendees to savor.

Zielona Góra's Święto Wina (Wine Festival) takes place in September. Attendees can taste a range of wines from both domestic and foreign producers.

International Street Art Festival: In July, Gdańsk organizes a lively street art event that highlights the skills of both domestic and foreign street artists.

In order to be sure you don't miss out on any fantastic festivals taking place in 2024, don't forget to check the precise dates, locations, and specifics of events closer to your planned visit. Have fun discovering the various cultural events Poland has to offer!

Polish Delights: Must-Try Recipes

Pierogi: Possibly the most recognizable dish from Poland. Pierogi are dumplings stuffed with a variety of fillings, including fruit, cheese, pork, potatoes, and mushrooms. They are frequently served with sour cream and can be baked, boiled, or fried.

Bigos: Also referred to as "Hunter's Stew," bigos is a filling dish prepared with fresh cabbage, sauerkraut, and a variety of meats, including bacon and sausage. For a deep, nuanced flavor, it is frequently cooked slowly.

Zurek: Served with sausage, potatoes, and hard-boiled eggs, Zurek is a sour rye soup. Though it's available all year round, it's usually savored around Easter.

Gołąbki: Typically baked in a tomato or mushroom sauce, gołąbki are cabbage rolls filled with a blend of minced meat, rice, and spices. They are a traditional Polish dish that is soothing.

Polish-style breaded and fried pork cutlet, akin to schnitzel, is called kotlet schabowy. It's frequently served with pickled cucumbers on the side and mashed potatoes.

Barszcz: Barszcz is a hot or cold soup made with beetroot. Sour cream and little dumplings known as "uszka" are frequently served with it. Barszcz has different regional variations.
Kielbasa: There are many different varieties and tastes of Polish sausage, or kielbasa. It is a mainstay of Polish cooking and can be eaten fresh, cured, or smoked. Savor it boiling, grilling, or adding it to stews and soups.

Similar to Italian gnocchi, kopytkas are traditional Polish potato dumplings. Typically, kopytka are served with a variety of toppings, including bacon, breadcrumbs, and fried onions.
Łazanki: Łazanki is a pasta meal that frequently includes cabbage, mushrooms, and occasionally meat. This dish is satisfying and hearty, ideal for individuals who want a taste of classic comfort food from Poland.

Makowiec: A well-liked treat in Poland, makowiec is a poppy seed roll filled with pulverized poppy seeds, honey, almonds, and occasionally raisins, baked in sweet dough. It is frequently savored on holidays.

Sernik: Made with quark or farmer's cheese, sernik is a classic Polish cheesecake. It is frequently garnished with fruit or a sprinkling of powdered sugar and can be flavored with citrus, chocolate, or vanilla.

For a genuinely traditional dining experience, don't forget to combine these delectable meals with a shot of vodka or a glass of Polish beer. Any trip to Poland must include sampling the local cuisine, as each region has its own specialties and a varied range of dishes.

Chapter Six: Historical Landmark

Royal Castles and Palaces

UNESCO has designated Wawel Castle (Zamek Królewski na Wawelu), which is situated in the center of Kraków, as a World Heritage Site. For centuries the kings and queens of Poland called it home. The Crown Treasury and Armory, State Rooms, and Royal Private Apartments are open for exploration by guests.

Warsaw's Royal Castle (Zamek Królewski):

The Royal Castle, the royal residence of Polish monarchs, was located in Warsaw's Old Town. It was rebuilt after World War II and today has a magnificent collection of decorative art, paintings, and sculptures housed within the museum.

One of the biggest mediaeval brick castles in the world, Malbork Castle (Zamek w Malborku) is located in Malbork and is recognized as a UNESCO World Heritage Site. The castle complex, which was first constructed by the Teutonic Knights, is a magnificent example of Gothic architecture and a reminder of the area's mediaeval past.

Warsaw's Wilanów Palace (Pałac w Wilanowie) is sometimes called the "Polish Versailles." Encircled by lovely grounds, it served as King John III Sobieski's summer home. A vast collection of artwork, including ornamental arts, sculptures, and paintings, is housed in the royal museum.

Nieborów: Nieborów Palace (Pałac w Nieborowie)
Nieborów Palace is a baroque home surrounded by a French-style garden, close to Warsaw. The palace is

home to a museum that features an exquisite collection of ceramics, furniture, and artwork.

Wałbrzych's Książ Castle (Zamek Książ):
One of the biggest castles in Poland is Książ Castle, which is located in Lower Silesia. Its history is complicated because it was home to several aristocratic families. The castle is a well-liked tourist site because of its lovely surroundings and gardens.
Pszczyna Castle, also known as Zamek w Pszczynie, is a stunning example of a castle and park complex designed in the romantic style. The castle, which is surrounded by a landscape park, has opulent interiors and hosts a variety of cultural events.

Lesna's Czocha Castle (Zamek Czocha) is a picturesque stronghold situated on Lake Leśniańskie in the southwest region of Poland. Its origins can be traced back to the thirteenth century, giving it a rich history. Visitors can explore the castle, and guided tours offer insights into its medieval design.

Ojców's Pieskowa Skała Castle (Zamek Pieskowa Skała):
The Ojców National Park is home to this Renaissance castle. It's a beautiful site because of its picturesque setting between vegetation and limestone rocks. A

branch of the Wawel Royal Castle Museum is located within the castle.

With their impressive architectural designs, priceless art collections, and historical significance, these royal castles and palaces provide a window into Poland's regal history. By visiting these locations, tourists can fully experience Poland's rich cultural and historical heritage.

Listed as World Heritage by UNESCO

Numerous UNESCO World Heritage Sites, chosen for their cultural and natural value, are located in Poland. The following are a few of Poland's noteworthy UNESCO World Heritage
Sites:

Wieliczka and Bochnia Royal Salt Mines: One of the oldest salt mines in the world currently in use is the Wieliczka Salt Mine, which is located close to Kraków. The mine has an intricate network of salt-carved tunnels, rooms, and chapels below ground. In addition to Wieliczka, another well-known salt mining location is Bochnia Salt Mine.

Concentration and Extermination Camps at Auschwitz-Birkenau: The camps serve as potent reminders of the Holocaust. The location provides proof of the systematic murder the Nazis committed during World War II.

Kraków's historic core is a UNESCO-listed monument that includes the Old Town, Wawel Castle, and Kazimierz, the city's old Jewish neighborhood. It displays the rich cultural and architectural legacy of the city.

Historic heart of Warsaw: After suffering significant damage during World War II, the historic heart of Warsaw was painstakingly rebuilt. Market Square, the Royal Castle, and other historically significant structures are all part of it.

Białowieża Forest: One of the largest and remaining remnants of the prehistoric forest that formerly covered most of Europe, Białowieża Forest is situated between Poland and Belarus. The European bison, a representation of the natural heritage of the continent, calls it home.

The Old City of Zamość is a finely built Renaissance city that is renowned for its intact architecture and urban design. The Italian Renaissance of the late sixteenth century left its mark on the Old City.

Wooden Churches of Southern Małopolska: Known for their distinctive architectural style and the cultural value they hold in the local communities, these wooden churches are spread throughout the Małopolska region and are included in the UNESCO site.

Bieszczady National Park is a well-known park in the Carpathian Mountains that boasts a variety of ecosystems, such as immaculate woods, meadows, and mountainous terrain.

Centennial Hall, situated in Wrocław, is a notable example of modernist architecture and an engineering wonder from the early 20th century. Max Berg, an architect, created it.

Muskauer Park, also known as Park Muzakowski, is a historic park that spans the border between Germany and Poland and features a landscape design that melds the two countries together harmoniously. It is a superb illustration of the craze for linked parks in the 19th century.

Poland is home to several UNESCO World Heritage Sites that highlight the rich cultural, historical, and environmental heritage of the nation. Investigating these sites reveals more about Poland's rich history and the importance of these amazing places around the world.

Chapter Seven: Outdoor Adventures

Exploring Poland's National Parks

Poland is endowed with a wide range of landscapes, and its national parks provide an opportunity to discover the rich natural beauty of the nation.

Podlaskie and Brest Regions are home to Białowieża National Park.

Highlights: The largest and final remnants of the ancient Białowieża Forest, recognized as a UNESCO World Heritage Site, can be found here. It is well-known for having a population of free-ranging European bison.

Tatra National Park, also known as Tatrański Park Narodowy, is situated in the Silesian Voivodeship in Lesser Poland.

Highlights: With its peaks, valleys, and pure lakes, the Tatra Mountains provide breathtaking alpine beauty. Hiking, rock climbing, and taking in the expansive vistas from mountain trails are popular pastimes.

Lesser known as Pieniny National Park (Pieniński Park Narodowy) Poland

Standouts: renowned for the Dunajec River Gorge, where tourists can ride traditional wooden rafts through breathtaking scenery. A notable feature is the Three Crowns Massif, and hiking paths provide amazing vistas.

West Pomeranian Voivodeship is home to Wolinski National Park, also known as Woliński Park Narodowy.

Highlights: Parts of the Baltic Sea and the island of Wolin are included in this park. It has a variety of topography, such as dunes, cliffs, and coastal marshes. The park is a birdwatcher's paradise.

Lesser Poland is home to Ojców National Park (Ojcowski Park Narodowy).

Standouts: Known for its limestone rock formations, caves, and the gorgeous Prądnik River Valley, Ojców is one of Poland's smallest national parks. Both plants and animals abound in the park.

Babia Góra National Park, also known as Babiogórski Park Narodowy, is situated in the Silesian Voivodeship and Lesser Poland.

Standouts: The highest point in the Beskid Mountains is Babia Góra. Alpine meadows and subalpine woods are two of the park's many ecosystems, and it has a variety of hiking trails.

Masovian Voivodeship is home to Kampinos National Park, also known as Kampinoski Park Narodowy.

Highlights: Kampinos, which is close to Warsaw, guards the Kampinoski Forest, which is a piece of the ancient forest that formerly covered the area. It's a great place to go birdwatching and on nature walks.

Lesser Poland is home to Gorce National Park (Gorczanski Park Narodowy).

Highlights: Gorce National Park is home to a wide range of plant and animal species, rolling hills, and dense woods. Hikers will find nirvana here, since there are designated pathways that lead to sweeping vistas.

Podlaskie Voivodeship is home to Biebrza National Park (Biebrzański Park Narodowy).

Standouts: The park, which is well-known for the Biebrza Marshes, is a birdwatcher's paradise, especially in the migration season. The meadows and marshes are home to a wide variety of species.

West Pomeranian Voivodeship is home to Drawa National Park (Drawieński Park Narodowy).

Highlights: The many lakes, rivers, and vast woodlands that make up Drawa National Park. Popular activities on the Drawa River include canoeing and kayaking, which offer a distinctive viewpoint of the park.

Discovering Poland's national parks is a great way to get in touch with the natural world, value biodiversity, and take in the varied topography of the nation—from wetlands and coastal regions to mountains and woods. Every park has a distinct character and offers outdoor enthusiasts a variety of recreational options.

Nature Trails and Hiking

There are several hiking and nature routes in Poland that help outdoor enthusiasts explore a variety of landscapes, from meadows and coastal areas to mountains and woods.

Tatra Mountains: Trail: There are a lot of hiking paths in the Tatra National Park, one of which is well-known and leads to the breathtaking alpine lake Morskie Oko. While lower regions offer more accessible pathways, the High Tatra region offers strenuous hikes for expert hikers.

Trail: Known for the Bieszczady National Park, the Bieszczady Mountains are located in the southeast. Beautiful scenery, such as broad meadows and deep forests, may be seen along the trails. One of the most popular treks is to the highest peak, Tarnica.

Karkonosze Mountains: Path: The routes in the Karkonosze National Park are varied, with the hike up Śnieżka being particularly noteworthy. Alpine meadows and unusual rock formations can be seen in the park.

Trail: The hiking paths in Babia Góra National Park, which is home to its namesake summit, are appropriate for hikers of all levels of experience. The trails offer expansive views as they wind through meadows and woodlands.

Ojców National Park: Trail: The scenic Prądnik River Valley, limestone formations, and caves may all be found on the trails in this park, which is close to Kraków. Historic castles are connected along the Eagle's Nests Trail.

Sand dunes that are constantly changing can be found in Słowiński National Park, which is located on the shore of the Baltic Sea. The Rowokół observation deck, which provides expansive views of the distinctive terrain, is reached by following the Red Trail.

routes in Gorce National Park: There are well-marked routes throughout the park that are appropriate for varying levels of fitness. A well-liked option that leads to the Gorce Mountains' highest peak is the Turbacz Trail.

Kampinos National Park: Trail: The Kampinos Forest is home to nature trails in Kampinos National Park, which is close to Warsaw. The park's long-distance trail winds through a variety of ecosystems in a picturesque manner.

Biebrza Marshes: paths: There are paths that go across marshes in the Podlaskie region's Biebrza National Park. There are several places to go birdwatching along the Red Trail, particularly in the migration seasons.

Drawa National Park: Trail: The Drawa River offers hiking and kayaking paths in this West Pomeranian national park. The Drawieński National Park Trail encompasses a variety of topographies.

Eagle's Nests Trail (Szlak Orlich Gniazd): Trail: This historic path links several fortifications and castles from the Middle Ages that are perched on limestone cliffs. It offers a blend of environment and history as it passes through the Kraków-Częstochowa Upland.

Primordial Beskid Trail (Main Beskid Trail): Trail Hikers can experience the splendor of the Beskid Mountains by traveling along this long-distance track that stretches across them. It includes a wide range of terrain, including pastoral valleys and mountain summits.

It's important to respect environment, be well-prepared, and observe route markers when exploring these trails. Poland's trails provide a wide variety of outdoor activities, whether you're looking for strenuous mountain treks or peaceful strolls in national parks.

Activities with Water

Poland provides a wide range of water sports for aficionados because to its many lakes, rivers, and coastline along the Baltic Sea.

Canoeing and Kayaking:

The rivers Biebrza, Krutynia, Drawa, and Czarna Hańcza are the locations.

Specifics: Poland offers a vast network of rivers that are ideal for canoeing and kayaking. Whether you're a novice or an expert paddler, you can take in the peace and quiet of the natural world while exploring beautiful scenery and wildlife.

Masurian Lake District is the location.

Details: Sailing aficionados will find the Masurian Lakes, sometimes referred to as the "Land of a Thousand Lakes," to be the ideal location. Take a guided sailing tour or rent a sailboat to explore the network of lakes and take in the gorgeous scenery.

Location: Baltic Sea Coast; spots like Sopot and the Hel Peninsula are good for windsurfing.

Details: The Baltic Sea coastline of Poland provides great windsurfing conditions. Experienced surfers can catch waves along the sandy beaches, and beginners can take training.

Location: Puck Bay, Hel Peninsula; kitesurfing available.

Details: The Hel Peninsula is a well-liked spot for kitesurfing because of its broad, sandy beaches and steady winds. For anyone interested in experiencing this exhilarating water sport, lessons and equipment rentals are offered.

Fishing spots: Biebrza River, Białowieża Forest, Lakes Mazury (Masuria).

Details: Fish abound in Poland's lakes and rivers, which makes it a top destination for anglers. Get a fishing license and try your hand at capturing trout, pike, and perch.

Swimming in the Baltic Sea: Places: Resorts and coastal cities (such as Gdańsk, Sopot, and Kolobrod).

Details: During the summer, you can unwind and swim at the sandy beaches along Poland's Baltic Sea coastline. A variety of water-related activities are available at coastal resorts, and the sea air offers a cooling respite.

Rafting in the Pieniny Mountains on the Dunajec River.

Details: Take in the breathtaking scenery as you raft down the Dunajec River, which meanders through the Pieniny Mountains. Through the breathtaking Dunajec Gorge, traditional wooden rafts are guided by knowledgeable guides.

The location of diving in the Baltic Sea is along its coast.

Details: Participate in diving activities to discover the Baltic Sea's underwater environment. Explore underwater formations, marine life, and shipwrecks.

Water Parks:

Locations: A number of cities, such as Kraków, Wrocław, and Warsaw.

Details: For family-friendly aquatic enjoyment, Poland is home to a number of water parks featuring slides, pools, and other attractions. Aqua Park Wrocław, Park Wodny Kraków, and Park Wodny Warsaw are a some of the well-known water parks.

Cruise along the Vistula River: Warsaw's Vistula River is the location.
Details: Enjoy beautiful views of Warsaw's skyline and historical sites by taking a leisurely ride along the Vistula River.
Prioritize safety first, follow local laws, and take the weather into account before participating in any water sports. Poland offers plenty to offer water fans, whether their preference is for the exhilaration of water sports or the tranquility of a serene lake.

Chapter Eighth: Local Experience

Shopping for Souvenirs

Amber Jewelry: A vast array of exquisitely carved amber jewelry, such as necklaces, bracelets, and earrings, may be found. Poland is known for its amber. Seek for pieces with a variety of hues and forms.

Bolesławiec Ceramics:

Bolesławiec is known for its unique ceramics, which frequently have elaborate patterns in white and blue. A range of dishes, bowls, and decorative things are available for selection.

Wycinanki (Cutouts from Paper):

Paper cutting, or wycinanki, is a traditional Polish craft. Paper cutouts with intricate designs frequently feature floral patterns, animals, and folk themes. A framed wycinanka would be a thoughtful and vibrant memento.

Pająki, or straw ornaments, are a typical Polish ornamental element that are frequently fashioned into vibrant chandeliers. They can bring a little bit of Polish tradition into your house and are linked to folk art.

Polish Pottery: Other Polish locations, including Bolesławiec, manufacture unique pottery. Seek out hand-painted pottery from places like Lublin and Zakopane that have a variety of patterns and vivid hues.

Oscypek Cheese: Traditionally made from smoked sheep's milk, oscypek is a distinctive memento from Poland's mountainous areas. It frequently arrives in ornamental wooden molds.

Kraków is well-known for its pierniki, or gingerbread cookies that are elaborately adorned. They come in a variety of tastes, sizes, and forms, and are frequently presented in adorable boxes.

Polish Vodka: There are many different brands and varieties to select from, and Poland is known for its vodka. Seek out distinctive and regionally made bottles, and think about bringing back a modest assortment to experience Polish spirits.

Polish Folk Costumes: Known as ethnic or regional costumes, traditional Polish folk costumes are unique and cultural mementos. They come in a variety of styles, each one reflecting a particular part of the nation.

Wooden Crafts: In Poland, hand-carved wooden objects including toys, figurines, and cooking utensils are popular gifts. Seek for handcrafted items with fine details and hints of Polish artistry.

Polish Delights:

Bring some foodie mementos, like jams and preserves from the area, Polish honey, or classic Polish candies like Ptasie Mleczko or Wedel chocolates.

Polish Folk Music and Instruments: Invest in classic CDs that feature Polish folk music or buy folk instruments like the dulcimer to bring a bit of Poland home.

To locate one-of-a-kind and genuine souvenirs, check out neighborhood markets, artisan stores, and craft fairs. Look for goods that showcase the distinct customs and cultural diversity of Poland's various regions.

Customary Folk Crafts and Art

Wycinanki (Paper Cutouts): Wycinanki is the Polish technique of cutting colored paper into elaborate designs. These cutouts, which depict the cultural legacy of various regions, frequently include geometric patterns, animals, flowers, and symbols.

Zalipie Painted Houses: The community of Zalipie, located in southeast Poland, is well-known for its custom of painting furniture, walls, and common objects with bright flower designs. Painted Easter eggs and ceramics in the Zalipie style are also well-liked.

Lowicz Embroidery and Cutouts: The Łowicz region is renowned for its elaborate embroidery and vibrant cutouts. Flowers, roosters, and geometric shapes are common elements of traditional designs. Seek out napkins, tablecloths, and costumes in the Łowicz style.

Bolesławiec Pottery: A special stamping method is used to manufacture the pottery, which is distinguished by patterns of blue and white. A variety of utensils, plates, bowls, and ornamental objects are included in the pottery.

Wood Carvings of the Gorals: The Gorals are a group of highlanders in the Tatra Mountains who are well-known for their unusual wood carvings. Traditional symbols, animals, and religious figures are frequently shown in these carvings. Seek out wooden utensils and sculptures.

Easter eggs decorated with elaborate designs, known as pisanki, are typically made using a wax-resist technique. Easter decorations are distinctive and vibrant since each location has its own designs and styles.

The colorful needlework of Kaszuby, a region in northern Poland, is well-known. Typical Kaszubian designs frequently include geometric shapes, florals, and foliage. It's typical to see Kaszubian embroidery on linens and clothes.

Goralski Style: The Tatra Mountains' ancient highland culture is embodied in the Goralski style. Seek out hand-carved wooden objects, leather goods, and fabrics with the characteristic Goral designs.

Furniture in the Zakopane Style: The mountain town of Zakopane is well-known for its distinctive wooden furniture design, which draws inspiration from the local highland architecture. Seek for intricately patterned hand-carved furniture.

Opoczno Ceramics: Known for their blue and white patterns, Opoczno ceramics are made in the village of Opoczno. Traditional pattern-adorned plates, bowls, and tiles are frequently seen in the pottery.

Lubelska Reductions:

Cutouts with exquisite lace-like designs are a common sight in Lublin and the Lubelskie region. Lubelska cutouts are a common decorative element found on walls and windows.

Kashubian Pottery: Known for its distinctive glazes and elaborate decorations, the pottery of the Kashubia region in northern Poland is highly recognized. Pottery from Kashubian tradition comprises bowls, plates, and ornamental pieces.

To support local artists and guarantee the authenticity of the pieces, take into consideration going to local markets, artisan workshops, and cultural events while buying traditional folk art and crafts. These handicrafts not only make exquisite decorations but also preserve Polish cultural tales and customs.

Getting Along with Locals

Learn Some Basic Polish words: Although many Poles, particularly in tourist destinations and bigger cities, may speak English, having a basic understanding of a few Polish words may help to promote goodwill. Speaking in their own tongue is often appreciated by the locals.

Be Respectful and Polite: In Polish society, being polite is highly regarded. Use courteous language; say "Dzień dobry" (good morning) to people, "Proszę" (please), and "Dziękuję" (thank you) when necessary.

Talk About tiny Things: In social settings, poles are prone to talking about tiny things. Safe bets include things like the local way of life, cuisine, and weather. Taking an authentic interest in their nation and customs might spark stimulating discussions.

Respect for Personal Space: Compared to some other cultures, poles may stand a little more apart during conversations because they value personal space. Save this space, and unless you have established a deep relationship, refrain from making excessively familiar gestures.

Take Part in Cultural Events: To interact with the community, go to local markets, festivals, or events. These events offer a chance to meet locals, discover customs, and maybe even take part in traditional dances or activities.

Sample Local Food: Eating together is a wonderful way to build relationships with locals. Visit neighborhood restaurants, pick up a discussion with servers or other patrons, and don't be afraid to ask for recommendations. Poles love to share their food with guests and take great pride in it.

Be Open-Minded: Be willing to accept cultural differences and approach conversations with an open mind. Respect the beliefs, customs, and traditions of the people you encounter, and make an effort to learn their point of view.

Visit Local Markets and Shops: To engage with sellers and artists, visit local markets and shops. You might find out fascinating facts about the things you're buying if you inquire about their merchandise.

Attend Social Gatherings: Take advantage of the chance to attend social gatherings, such as neighborhood get-togethers, birthday parties, or neighborhood meetings. People from Poland are usually kind to outsiders who express interest in their neighborhood.

Take Public Transportation: Seeing local life up close is made possible by using public transportation. On the bus or train, strike up a discussion with other travelers or inquire about recommendations from the locals.

Recognize Cultural Sensitivities: Keep in mind that certain cultures have strong feelings about certain historical periods. For instance, discussing subjects pertaining to World War II can be delicate, so proceed with caution.

Show Your Appreciation: Let someone know how much you appreciate them if they go above and beyond to assist you or supply you information. Saying "dziękuję" (thank you) is really helpful.

Your contacts with the amiable people of Poland are sure to be good and unforgettable if you approach them with openness, respect, and a sincere interest in the local way of life.

Chapter Nine: Practical Tips

Safety Guidelines

Emergency Numbers: Write down or memorize emergency numbers, such as 112, which is Poland's general emergency number, as well as the precise contacts for the local police, ambulance, and consulate.
Remain Up to Date:
Stay up to date on the latest local news, the weather, and any possible safety issues. Make use of reliable news outlets and official travel advisories.

Safeguard Your belongings: Be cautious when traveling by public transit and in busy areas to prevent being pickpocketed. Put valuables in a safe location and use anti-theft bags.

Use Licensed Transportation: Make sure to use trustworthy and licensed companies while taking cabs or other forms of transportation. Make sure the taxi is equipped with a meter or decide on a fare in advance of the trip.

Be Wary at Night: Take extra care when strolling by yourself at night, particularly in uncharted or dimly lighted places. Stay on well-lit, well-traveled routes.

Respect Local legislation: Become knowledgeable about the rules and legislation that apply in your area. Regarding the use of illegal drugs and public intoxication, Poland maintains strong restrictions. Always follow the law when driving, and be aware of regional traditions.

Health Precautions: Make sure your regular immunizations are current and think about getting additional shots, like hepatitis A and B. Keep your health insurance card and any essential medications with you.

Secure Hostels:

Select trustworthy lodging that has received positive evaluations. Make sure appropriate security measures are in place at your hotel or guesthouse. Use the hotel safe for important belongings.

Recognize Your Environment:

Get acquainted with the design of the city or region you are visiting. Know where your consulate or embassy is located, where the closest hospitals are, and where emergency services are located.

Use ATMs Carefully: Exercise caution when utilizing ATMs, particularly in remote or dimly lit locations. Use ATMs found in safe havens or banks, and cover your PIN when entering it.
Invest in comprehensive travel insurance that covers theft, trip cancellations, and medical situations. Keep a copy of your insurance policy and your emergency contact information on you.
Cultural Sensitivity: Honor regional traditions and customs. It might not be appropriate in some places to take pictures of specific people or places without permission. Prior to taking a picture, always ask.

Keep Yourself Hydrated: Especially in the warmer months, keep yourself hydrated. Drink from reliable sources and have a reusable water bottle with you.
Public transit Safety: Exercise caution and pay attention to your surroundings when using public transit. Keep a watch on your possessions and notify the authorities of any questionable conduct.

COVID-19 Precautions: Keep up with the most recent COVID-19 guidelines and heed the advice to take protective precautions, such as mask wearing and social separation. Recognize any limitations or prerequisites for entry.

Keep in mind that safety might change based on the particular setting and conditions, so exercise caution and good judgment at all times. Do not hesitate to contact your embassy or local authorities for assistance in case of an emergency or with any concerns.

Information about Health and Emergencies

Emergency Services: In Poland, 112 is the general emergency number. You can call this number in case of fire, medical, or police emergency.

Poland boasts a sophisticated healthcare system that includes state-of-the-art medical facilities. For non-urgent medical concerns, you can go to nearby clinics or hospitals. For basic medical treatment, residents of the European Union may utilize the European Health Insurance Card (EHIC).

Travel Insurance: Having comprehensive travel insurance that covers medical emergencies, trip cancellations, and other unanticipated situations is highly advised. Keep a copy of your insurance policy and your emergency contact information on you.

Vaccinations: Before visiting Poland, make sure your usual immunizations are current. Think about getting extra immunizations, such hepatitis A and B, depending on your schedule and medical history.

Food and Water Safety: Although tap water in Poland is usually safe to drink, you can always get bottled water if you're concerned. Choose trustworthy restaurants and use caution when it comes to food hygiene. Steer clear of undercooked or raw meat and seafood.

Medical Facilities: English-speaking physicians and well-equipped medical facilities can be found in Poland's major cities. It's advisable to have a basic comprehension of the local language or have a translation tool, as medical services may be more restricted in rural areas.

Medication: Pack plenty of any prescription drugs you might require for the duration of your visit. Carrying a modest first aid kit with necessary items like bandages, painkillers, and any OTC meds you might need is also a smart idea.

Information about COVID-19: Remain current on the most recent COVID-19 regulations and limitations. Take all advised precautions, including as mask wearing and social isolation. Recognize any admittance requirements or testing procedures that may exist.

Health precautions: Wash your hands frequently and maintain proper hygiene to stop the transmission of infection. In situations where soap and water are unavailable, have hand sanitizer on hand.

Protection from Insects: Use insect repellent to ward off ticks, mosquitoes, and other insects if you want to spend time outside, particularly in rural or wooded locations.

Food allergies, in particular, should be disclosed to restaurant personnel. You should also carry any necessary drugs, such as an auto-injector for epinephrine or antihistamines.

Altitude Considerations: Be mindful of any potential problems related to altitude if you intend to travel to hilly areas. If you're going to be traveling to higher altitudes, take modest steps to acclimate yourself.

Local Pharmacies: Over-the-counter drugs and health advice can be obtained from pharmacists in Poland, where pharmacies, or apteka, are widely located. It can be useful to be aware of the generic names for medications that are sold under different brand names.

In the event of an emergency, know the location and phone number of your embassy. They are able to help with emergency evacuation in the event of a catastrophic emergency.

You can make sure you have a safe and healthy vacation to Poland by being aware and taking the appropriate precautions. For specific recommendations based on your unique health needs and travel schedule, always visit medical professionals or travel health clinics.

Essentials for Packing

Bring outfits that are appropriate for the weather when you arrive. It's best to dress in layers because temperatures can change. For wet days, pack a waterproof jacket.

suitable Shoes: If you intend to explore cities or engage in outdoor activities, make sure you pack suitable walking shoes.

Formal Attire: You might want to bring formal clothing if you're going to fancy restaurants or special events.

Swimwear: Bring swimwear if your plan calls for visits to beaches or lodgings with pools.

Sun Protection: To shield yourself from the sun, wear a wide-brimmed hat, sunglasses, and sunscreen.

Travel documents include your passport, visa (if needed), proof of insurance, and any relevant permissions.

Payment options include credit/debit cards, local Polish złoty currencies, and modest amounts of cash.

Travel adapters and chargers are essential for charging electrical devices such as phones, cameras, and other electronics.

Travel blanket and pillow: These are helpful for extended flights or road trips, particularly if you intend to sleep.

Prescription Drugs: If you think you might need any prescription drugs while traveling, make sure you have plenty with you.

First Aid Kit: Standard first aid supplies, such as painkillers, bandages, disinfectant wipes, and any prescription drugs.

Apply insect repellent: This is particularly crucial if you intend to spend time in rural or forested areas.

Personal care products: toothpaste, shampoo, conditioner, toothbrush, and any other items needed for personal hygiene.

Travel-Sized Laundry Detergent: This is helpful if you intend to do laundry while traveling or for longer excursions.

Travel Towel: For ease when traveling, a compact, fast-drying towel.

Smartphone and Accessories: A portable charger, your smartphone, and any additional accessories you might require.

Camera: Make sure you have a dedicated camera and extra memory cards if that's what you prefer.

If required for business or leisure activities during downtime, a laptop or tablet.

Other Items:

Daypacks or small backpacks are handy for carrying necessities on day trips and freeing up your hands.

reusable Water bottle: Refill your bottle throughout the day to stay hydrated.

A notebook and pen are useful for recording addresses, ideas, and notes while traveling.

An umbrella that is small and convenient to carry for sudden downpours of rain.

Comfort and Entertainment: Comfortable entertainment for long trips or idleness.

Travel locks: Locks to protect your belongings and bags.

Non-perishable snacks to keep you going between meals or while traveling.

Don't forget to modify this list according to the particular activities you have in mind and the time of year you will be visiting. Make sure you are ready for the weather during your trip to Poland by checking the local weather prediction.

CONCLUSION

Every location offers a different tapestry of customs, delectable foods, and breathtaking natural features, from the historic alleys of Warsaw to the captivating vistas of the Tatra Mountains. You will have a greater understanding of Poland's history through engaging with locals, enjoying regional cuisine, and taking part in cultural activities.

By following local regulations, being aware of emergency services, and taking common sense safeguards, you may ensure your safety. When packing, take into account the climate, cultural norms, and the things you have planned to do.

Poland welcomes you to make lifelong experiences, whether you're exploring historic towns, taking leisurely hikes, or reveling in the creative gems of Kraków. I hope your trip is full of joy, discovery, and a sincere appreciation of Poland's beauty as you visit its UNESCO World Heritage Sites, eat mouthwatering pierogi, and engage with its lively customs. Happy travels!

Printed in Great Britain
by Amazon